The

Anglican-Roman Catholic

Agreement

on the

Eucharist

The 1971 Anglican-Roman Catholic Statement on the Eucharist

with

An Historical Introduction and Theological Commentary

Julian W. Charley

Vicar of St. Peter's Church, Everton, Liverpool
Member of the Anglican-Roman Catholic International Commission

GROVE BOOKS
BRAMCOTE   NOTTS.

CONTENTS

The Statement on the Eucharist Copyright the Anglican-Roman Catholic International Commission.

Historical Introduction and Theological Commentary Copyright Julian W. Charley 1971 and 1972

First Edition December 1971
Second Edition May 1972
Reprinted November 1973
Reprinted November 1975

The quotation from *Growing into Union* (by C. O. Buchanan, E. L. Mascall, J. I. Packer and the Bishop of Willesden, S.P.C.K. London, 1970) on page 18 is reprinted by kind permission of the publishers.

ISSN 0305 3067
ISBN 0 901710 16 4

PREFACE

Any claim by Anglicans and Roman Catholics to have reached agreement on such a subject as the eucharist will inevitably be scrutinised very minutely. Yet to reduce the long-term thinking of a Commission to such a brief compass as in the present Statement makes for difficulties, so that the full significance of what is said may still escape recognition. It is to assist the reader to understand in greater depth the implications of the Commission's work that this booklet has been written. It sets out the agreed Statement, together with both a survey of the historical background to the Statement and a Theological Commentary on its contents.

Within the framework of the Commission's substantial agreement, there is obviously room for some breadth of interpretation. Whereas the Statement itself is the unanimous conclusion of the whole Commission, a commentary, even when it comes from a member of the Commission, must necessarily express a personal viewpoint. However, the author has consulted both Chairmen during the writing of the booklet, and has endeavoured to meet their desires over any points that they have raised. While their patient help is gratefully acknowledged, the author himself takes sole responsibility for the final product.

Julian W. Charley
16th December, 1971

PREFACE TO SECOND EDITION

In the light of the large amount of critical comment generated by the publication of the Statement, I have carefully re-examined my original Introduction and Commentary. As a result I have added two footnotes to the Introduction and one to the Commentary, changed a few words in the Commentary itself and added two brief passages. Apart from this, I have let it stand unchanged. I must here acknowledge Bishop Clark's kindness in letting me see his forthcoming Commentary *Agreement on the Eucharist* (to be published by the Roman Catholic Ecumenical Commission of England and Wales). I have not been able to comment here on the details of his Commentary (which is obviously designed to meet the anxieties of some Roman Catholics), but I am glad to have the chance to weigh Bishop Clark's words before putting my own booklet out into print again.

In general the members of the Commission seem to have been gratified by the reception accorded to the Statement, and this is a spur to our further endeavours.

Julian W. Charley
28th April, 1972

3

1. HISTORICAL INTRODUCTION

THE GREAT DIVIDE

The division that split the Western Church in the sixteenth century into Catholic and Protestant camps was undoubtedly the outcome of a most complex development. Historians may ascribe it to numerous causes, but that a deep doctrinal divergence lay at the heart of it is certain. Even in England, where a political break with Rome largely preceded the theological reformation, ultimately it was sealed by irreconcilable doctrinal disagreement. The Council of Trent only confirmed the parting of the ways. Yet even in that turbulent period there were eminent theologians on both sides who still believed that a *rapprochement* might be possible. For instance, at the Colloquy of Ratisbon in 1541 the participants achieved agreement on the highly controversial subject of justification, only to be denounced by those they represented as guilty of betrayal. Admittedly the participants were few, but they proved that something could be accomplished. Today historians are increasingly recognizing the importance of the views held by minorities in the great eras of controversy[1]. Perhaps the sixteenth century peace-makers were sometimes nearer the mark than the more renowned representatives of Catholic and Protestant orthodoxy. Certainly, the ability of recent historians to examine dispassionately the great controversies of the past has made possible a substantial reappraisal of history. Consequently ecumenical dialogue today can turn more readily to the shared concerns of the present without necessarily being trapped in the morass of sixteenth century debate.

ANGLICAN-ROMAN RELATIONS

Anglican-Roman relations in the last four hundred years have had a chequered career. The excommunication of Elizabeth I by the Pope left English Catholics in an embarrassing position, whereby loyalty to their sovereign and loyalty to their faith were placed in conflict. The Franciscan Sancta Clara in the seventeenth century reinterpreted the Thirty-Nine Articles in a Catholic sense, somewhat anticipating Newman's Tract XC; but all his striving for reunion proved abortive. Despite Catholic sympathies Anglicans such as William Laud and Jeremy Taylor tended to find themselves more in confrontation than in agreement. It was not so much the Civil War and the triumph of Puritanism that terminated the possibility of improved relations but the expulsion of James II in 1688 for trying to bring in Catholicism upon his subjects. With the coming of William III to the throne Protestantism was firmly written into the English Constitution. A century of Jacobite intrigue followed, which prevented any further negotiations until the nineteenth century, apart from one brief

---

[1] See Giuseppe Alberigo, *New Frontiers in Church History*, in *Concilium* Vol. 7, No. 6 (Sept. 1970), pp. 68-84.

interlude. From 1717 to 1720 Archbishop Wake negotiated with representatives of Gallicanism for the reunion of the Church of England with the French Church—an ambitious scheme that came to nothing. Eventually cooler heads and some political expediency brought about Catholic Emancipation in England in 1829. Then in 1865 E. B. Pusey produced his first *Eirenicon* in which he argued that division was caused more by the unofficial devotions and popular misconceptions of the Catholic Church than by its official teaching. It was an elaborate defence of the English Church in reply to a polemical pamphlet of Archbishop Manning together with a suggested basis for reunion with Rome. Further overtures by Pusey were abruptly halted by the declaration on Papal Infallibility at the Vatican Council of 1870.

1870-1960

Negotiations opened up again when Lord Halifax, president of the English Church Union, visited the Pope in Rome in 1894 and initiated discussions on the Catholic validity of Anglican orders. However, the result was the papal encyclical *Apostolicae Curae* two years later, which pronounced Anglican orders to be 'absolutely null and utterly void'. Once again it appeared that a total *impasse* had been reached. But not even this rebuff would daunt Lord Halifax. Encouraged in part by the 1920 Lambeth 'Appeal to all Christian People' for reunion, the elderly Viscount reopened the matter with Cardinal Mercier, which led to the setting-up in 1921 of the Malines Conversations. They were undertaken with the knowledge of Archbishop Davidson and the Pope, but without official sponsoring. Caution was the order of the day. The fact that the first meeting was kept secret till afterwards gave the Conversations an unfortunate cloak-and-dagger appearance. Moreover, the Anglican members were all staunch Anglo-Catholics, though not all were enamoured of the Papacy. Inevitably such an unrepresentative group aroused considerable alarm in Anglican Protestant circles, for they appeared ready to make concessions that were wholly unacceptable to many fellow-Anglicans. English Roman Catholics were also concerned because they had not been consulted. Ultimately the death of Cardinal Mercier in 1926 brought the Conversations to an inconclusive end and Pius XI's encyclical *Mortalium Animos* (1928) put a damper on Catholic participation in any further ecumenical ventures. So matters stood till the death of Pius XII and the private visit of Archbishop Fisher to Pope John in 1960.

VATICAN II

The second Vatican Council opened an entirely new era. The Decree on Ecumenism, while deploring 'a false conciliatory approach', advocated dialogue with other Christians.

"The manner and order in which Catholic belief is expressed should in no way become an obstacle to dialogue with our brethren" (11).

The same paragraph went on to speak of a 'hierarchy' of truths[1], determined by their relationship to the foundation of the Christian faith. Anglicans have long differentiated between fundamentals and non-fundamentals,

[1] On the background to the now celebrated phrase see Bernard Leeming, *The Vatican Council and Christian Unity* (D.L.T., 1966) Appendix VII, pp. 298-9.

5

so that this pointed to the possibility of a real dialogue that could be genuinely mutual. The document also speaks not only of 'separated brethren' but of 'churches and ecclesial communites separated from the Roman apostolic see'. The acknowledgement of separated 'churches' was a significant advance. In speaking of divisions in the West the Decree states,

> "Among those in which some Catholic traditions and institutions continue to exist, the Anglican Communion occupies a special place" (13).

Such a change of climate led to the official visit of the present Archbishop of Canterbury to Pope Paul VI in Rome in 1966. The Archbishop has made no secret of his desire to see the long-standing breach between the two Communions healed. Pope Paul has expressed a similar concern. In the same year Cardinal Heenan spoke of the need for Roman Catholics to talk not just to Anglo-Catholic Anglicans but also to Evangelicals: the error of Malines should not be repeated. The Church of England Evangelical Council contacted the Cardinal and they jointly established regular theological talks between Catholics and Evangelical Anglicans in England.

THE TALKS

In the meantime much wider plans were afoot. At their meeting the Archbishop and the Pope had decided to set up an Anglican-Roman Catholic Joint Preparatory Commission, which duly began its series of three meetings in 1967. A representative cross-section was sought in the appointment of the membership of each team. The function of this Commission was to evolve a programme for dialogue and co-operation, which was set out in the Malta Report of 1968, a document which it was decided not to publish. However, it was leaked in the *Tablet* of 29th November, 1968, and hence became common knowledge. In its recommendations it spoke of 'our quest for the full, organic unity of our two Communions'.

Following the publication of the Malta Report, a new Commission, entitled the Anglican-Roman Catholic International Commission (ARCIC), was appointed in 1969 by the Archbishop of Canterbury, in consultation with the Lambeth Consultative Body, and by the Vatican Secretariat for Christian Unity. The original title of *Permanent* was changed to *International* to avoid the suggestion of an interminable discussion until the Parousia! Its work began in Windsor in January 1970, with the programme recommended by the Preparatory Commission before it. Each Communion has nine delegates and a secretary. Consultants are also invited and there is an observer from the World Council of Churches. A list of the delegates can be found on pages 12 and 13.

For the most part the membership is drawn from across the English-speaking countries of the world, spanning the theological spectrum in each Communion: for example, the Anglican members range from the Anglo-Catholic Bishop of Pretoria in South Africa to the present writer, a conservative Evangelical from England. The differences of theology and outlook have proved to be just as marked among Roman Catholics as among Anglicans—an important indication that we both live for better or worse in churches that are *de facto* comprehensive.

The Commission meets annually for a week's conference. At Windsor guide-line papers were read in plenary session and then three sub-commission groups were formed, to tackle the questions of Authority, Ministry and Eucharist respectively. The work of sub-commissions has continued in between the main meetings and it has been that concerned with the Eucharist in which I have been involved. By the time of the second main meeting at Venice in September 1970 each sub-commission was beginning to make some headway. It was generally felt desirable for the sake of the Commission's credibility and to promote wider discussions to publish something, even if only working papers, at the end of this meeting, though a minority felt this to be premature. The difficulty lay in the lack of time for ironing out uneven or misleading elements in the three working papers submitted to the plenary session at the end. On the understanding that it would be possible for members to submit brief critical notes which would be appended to these working papers, all then gave approval to the proposal to publish. At this juncture there was an administrative mishap concerning publication. Combined and individual critical notes were submitted under the names of Fr. J. M. R. Tillard, a Dominican working in Canada, and myself. When publication took place in England in February 1971 in *Theology* and the *Clergy Review*, the notes were not included. The papers were entitled 'Church and Authority', 'Church and Eucharist' and 'Church and Ministry'. However, it was emphasized that these were only working papers and did not carry the unanimous approval of every member of the Commission. Not surprisingly they were not warmly received. Their lack of definitive status made them difficult to evaluate. With the benefit of hindsight one might feel that the coincidence of their publication with the height of the English postal strike, which meant that they were accorded comparatively little attention, was ultimately gain rather than loss.

THE NEW STATEMENT ON THE EUCHARIST

At Venice it was decided to devote the following year's work to a concentrated study of the eucharist. The original sub-commission on this theme met again in spring '71 in Norfolk. The unsatisfactory nature of the published paper along with the mishap attending its production, which made it less than fully representative of the Commission's mind, caused the sub-commission to make a new start. Large areas of the document were excised, other parts re-written and fresh matter incorporated. This new statement became the working basis for the next main meeting of the Commission in September 1971 at Windsor. In the meantime a most important article appeared in *Nouvelle Revue Theologique* for June-July '71, entitled 'Catholiques romains et Anglicans: l'Eucharistie' by Fr. Tillard. With a thorough understanding of the writings and particular concerns of Evangelicals as well as Catholics in the Church of England, the author indicated lines of convergence that suggested a way forward in theological agreement. Allusion was made to the doctrinal section of *Growing into Union* (Buchanan et al., SPCK, 1970) where Anglo-Catholic and Evangelical scholars had succeeded in achieving a considerable measure of agreement without compromising their basic convictions. These developments were an auspicious preliminary to the Windsor meeting.

The culmination of that meeting was the attaining of an agreement on eucharistic doctrine. The press release stated that a consensus had been reached and that the agreed statement would be published shortly. Delay was inevitable because of the need to refer back the Commission's conclusions to the appointing authorities. Nevertheless, to make public the fact of an agreement without the agreed document itself was to invite incredulity and alarmist speculation, which in some quarters duly ensued.

It should be noted that the Statement binds no-one bar the signatories. It will carry no specific authority in either Church. Moreover, only the eucharist is dealt with, and that not exhaustively. The coming year is to be devoted to the subject of the ministry, while some other doctrines are not even on the future agenda. Consequently it is necessary to see what has been achieved in this wider context. It has been with this end in view that this present theological commentary has been written, a personal commendation of the Statement by an individual member of the Commission with the full cognizance of the Anglican and Roman Catholic chairmen.

The theological progress made since the opening of the discussions has been an exhilarating experience, though often encountering set-backs and temporary deadlock. Without a doubt the atmosphere of growing mutual trust and friendship among the delegates has contributed greatly to the advance. Moreover, it is within this experienced fellowship that the pain of not being able to share together around the Lord's Table is most acutely felt. It is to be hoped that this Statement will prove a step towards the healing of our divisions.

2. THE STATEMENT OF THE EUCHARIST

ANGLICAN/ROMAN CATHOLIC INTERNATIONAL COMMISSION

Third Meeting, Windsor, 7th September, 1971

AGREED STATEMENT ON EUCHARISTIC DOCTRINE

INTRODUCTION

The following Agreed Statement evolved from the thinking and the discussion of the International Commission over the past two years. The result has been a conviction among members of the Commission that we have reached agreement on essential points of Eucharistic doctrine. We are equally convinced ourselves that, though no attempt was made to present a fully comprehensive treatment of the subject, nothing essential has been omitted. The document has been presented to our official authorities, but obviously it cannot be ratified by them until such time as our respective Churches can evaluate its conclusion.

We would want to point out that the members of the Commission who subscribed to this Statement have been officially appointed and come from many countries, representing a wide variety of theological background. Our intention was to reach a consensus at the level of faith, so that all of us might be able to say, within the limits of the Statement: this is the Christian faith of the Eucharist.

HENRY OSSORY
ALAN ELMHAM
Co-Chairmen

9

THE STATEMENT

1.   In the course of the Church's history several traditions have developed in expressing christian understanding of the eucharist. (For example, various names have become customary as descriptions of the eucharist: lord's supper, liturgy, holy mysteries, synaxis, mass, holy communion. The eucharist has become the most universally accepted term.) An important stage in progress towards organic unity is a substantial consensus on the purpose and meaning of the eucharist. Our intention has been to seek a deeper understanding of the reality of the eucharist which is consonant with biblical teaching and with the tradition of our common inheritance, and to express in this document the consensus we have reached.

2.   Through the life, death and resurrection of Jesus Christ God has re-conciled men to himself, and in Christ he offers unity to all mankind. By his word God calls us into a new relationship with himself as our Father and with one another as his children—a relationship inaugurated by baptism into Christ through the Holy Spirit, nurtured and deepened through the eucharist, and expressed in a confession of one faith and a common life of loving service.

I. THE MYSTERY OF THE EUCHARIST

3.   When his people are gathered at the eucharist to commemorate his saving acts for our redemption, Christ makes effective among us the eternal benefits of his victory and elicits and renews our response of faith, thanksgiving and self-surrender. Christ through the Holy Spirit in the eucharist builds up the life of the church, strengthens its fellowship and furthers its mission. The identity of the church as the body of Christ is both expressed and effectively proclaimed by its being centred in, and partaking of, his body and blood. In the whole action of the eucharist, and in and by his sacramental presence given through bread and wine, the crucified and risen Lord, according to his promise, offers himself to his people.

4.   In the eucharist we proclaim the Lord's death until he comes. Receiving a foretaste of the kingdom to come, we look back with thanksgiving to what Christ has done for us, we greet him present among us, we look forward to his final appearing in the fullness of his kingdom when "The Son also himself [shall] be subject unto him that put all things under him, that God may be all in all" (1 Cor. 15: 28). When we gather around the same table in this communal meal at the invitation of the same Lord and when we "partake of the one loaf", we are one in commitment not only to Christ and to one another, but also to the mission of the church in the world.

II. THE EUCHARIST AND THE SACRIFICE OF CHRIST

5.   Christ's redeeming death and resurrection took place once and for all in history. Christ's death on the cross, the culmination of his whole life of obedience, was the one, perfect and sufficient sacrifice for the sins of the world. There can be no repetition of or addition to what was then accomplished once for all by Christ. Any attempt to express a nexus between the sacrifice of Christ and the eucharist must not obscure this fundamental fact of the christian faith.[1] Yet God has given the eucharist to his church as a means through which the atoning work of Christ on the cross is proclaimed and made effective in the life of the church. The notion of *memorial* as understood in the passover celebration at the time of Christ—i.e. the making effective in the present of an event in the past— has opened the way to a clearer understanding of the relationship between Christ's sacrifice and the eucharist. The eucharistic memorial is no mere calling to mind of a past event or of its significance, but the church's effectual proclamation of God's mighty acts. Christ instituted the eucharist as a memorial (*anamnesis*) of the totality of God's reconciling action in him. In the eucharistic prayer the church continues to make a perpetual memorial of Christ's death, and his members, united with God and one another, give thanks for all his mercies, entreat the benefits of his passion on behalf of the whole church, participate in these benefits and enter into the movement of his self-offering.

III. THE PRESENCE OF CHRIST

6.   Communion with Christ in the eucharist presupposes his true presence, effectually signified by the bread and wine which, in this mystery, become his body and blood.[2] The real presence of his body and blood can, however, only be understood within the context of the redemptive activity whereby he gives himself, and in himself reconciliation, peace and life, to his own. On the one hand, the eucharistic gift springs out of the paschal mystery of Christ's death and resurrection, in which God's saving purpose has already been definitively realised. On the other hand, its purpose is to transmit the life of the crucified and risen Christ to his body, the church, so that its members may be more fully united wih Christ and with one another.

7.   Christ is present and active, in various ways, in the entire eucharistic celebration. It is the same Lord who through the proclaimed word invites

[1]   The early church in expressing the meaning of Christ's death and resurrection often used the language of sacrifice. For the Hebrew *sacrifice* was a traditional means of communication with God. The passover, for example, was a communal meal; the day of Atonement was essentially expiatory; and the covenant established communion between God and man.

[2]   The word *transubstantiation* is commonly used in the Roman Catholic Church to indicate that God acting in the eucharist effects a change in the inner reality of the elements. The term should be seen as affirming the *fact* of Christ's presence and of the mysterious and radical change which takes place. In contemporary Roman Catholic theology it is not understood as explaining *how* the change takes place.

11

his people to his table, who through his minister presides at that table, and who gives himself sacramentally in the body and blood of his paschal sacrifice. It is the Lord present at the right hand of the Father, and therefore transcending the sacramental order, who thus offers to his church, in the eucharistic signs the special gift of himself.

8.   The sacramental body and blood of the Saviour are present as an offering to the believer awaiting his welcome. When this offering is met by faith, a lifegiving encounter results. Through faith Christ's presence— which does not depend on the individual's faith in order to be the Lord's real gift of himself to his church—becomes no longer just a presence *for* the believer, but also a presence *with* him. Thus, in considering the mystery of the eucharistic presence, we must recognise both the sacramental sign of Christ's presence and the personal relationship between Christ and the faithful which arises from that presence.

9.   The Lord's words at the last supper, "Take and eat; this is my body," do not allow us to dissociate the gift of the presence and the act of sacramental eating. The elements are not mere signs; Christ's body and blood become really present and are really given. But they are really present and given in order that, receiving them, believers may be united in communion with Christ the Lord.

10.   According to the traditional order of the liturgy the consecratory prayer (*anaphora*) leads to the communion of the faithful. Through this prayer of thanksgiving, a word of faith addressed to the Father, the bread and wine become the body and blood of Christ by the action of the Holy Spirit, so that in communion we eat the flesh of Christ and drink his blood.

11.   The Lord who thus comes to his people in the power of the Holy Spirit is the Lord of glory. In the eucharistic celebration we anticipate the joys of the age to come. By the transforming action of the Spirit of God, earthly bread and wine become the heavenly manna and the new wine, the eschatological banquet for the new man: elements of the first creation become pledges and first fruits of the new heaven and the new earth.

*   *   *   *   *   *

12.   We believe that we have reached substantial agreement on the doctrine of the eucharist. Although we are all conditioned by the traditional ways in which we have expressed and practised our eucharistic faith, we are convinced that if there are any remaining points of disagreement they can be resolved on the principles here established. We acknowledge a variety of theological approaches within both our communions. But we have seen it as our task to find a way of advancing together beyond the doctrinal disagreements of the past. It is our hope that in view of the agreement which we have reached on eucharistic faith, this doctrine will no longer constitute an obstacle to the unity we seek.

Anglican delegates

The Rt. Revd. H. R. McAdoo,
      Bishop of Ossory, Ferns and Leighlin (Co-Chairman)
The Most Revd. F. R. Arnott,
      Archbishop of Brisbane

The Rt. Revd. J. R. H. Moorman,
  Bishop of Ripon
The Rt. Revd. E. G. Knapp-Fisher,
  Bishop of Pretoria
The Very Revd. Henry Chadwick,
  Dean of Christ Church, Oxford
The Revd. J. W. Charley,
  Vice-Principal, St. John's College, Nottingham
The Revd. Professor Eugene Fairweather,
  Keble Professor of Divinity, Trinity College, University of Toronto
The Revd. Professor H. E. Root,
  Professor of Theology, University of Southampton
The Rt. Revd. A. A. Vogel,
  Bishop-Coadjutor of West Missouri

Consultants

The Revd. Dr. R. J. Halliburton, Tutor, St. Stephen's House, Oxford
The Revd. Dr. H. R. Smythe, Director, Anglican Centre, Rome

Secretary

The Revd. Colin Davey, Assistant General Secretary, Church of England
  Council on Foreign Relations

Roman Catholic delegates

The Rt. Revd. Alan Clark,
  Auxiliary Bishop of Northampton (Co-Chairman)
The Rt. Revd. Christopher Butler, O.S.B.
  Auxiliary Bishop of Westminster
The Revd. Fr. Herbert Ryan, S.J.
  Professor of Historical Theology, Pontifical Faculty of Theology,
  Woodstock College, New York
Professor J. J. Scarisbrick,
  Professor of History, University of Warwick
The Revd. Georges Tavard, A.A.
  Professor of Theology, Methodist Theological School, Delaware
The Revd. F. Jean M. R. Tillard, O.P.
  Professor of Dogmatic Theology in Dominican Faculty of Theology,
  Ottawa
The Revd. Fr. P. Duprey, W.F.
  Under Secretary, Vatican Secretariat for Promoting Christian Unity
The Revd. Fr. E. J. Yarnold, S.J.
  Master, Campion Hall, Oxford
The Revd. Fr. Barnabas Ahern, C.P.
  Professor of Sacred Scripture, Rome
  —was unable to attend the Windsor meeting, 1971

Secretary

The Very Revd. Canon W. A. Purdy,
  Staff Member of the Vatican Secretariat for Promoting Christian Unity

World Council of Churches Observer

The Revd. Dr. Gunther Gassmann,
  Research Professor at the Centre d'Etudes Oecumeniques, Strasbourg

3. THEOLOGICAL COMMENTARY

Figures in parentheses, e.g. '(2)', refer to the sections of the Statement printed above on pages 10—12

From the very beginning of the Christian church it is evident that those who had been baptized into Christ met to share in the breaking of bread. It was their characteristic act. To try to live as a Christian without the Lord's supper would have been unthinkable, even though pressure of circumstances might sometimes have denied the opportunity. At the Lord's supper the significance of their baptism was expressed and lived out. Here was brought into focus the whole compass of God's salvation. Here was sustained the Christian's union with his Lord and with his fellow-members of Christ's body. No wonder this was the characteristic act of the first disciples, and such it has continued to be for subsequent generations. It is all the more tragic, therefore, when Christians so diverge from one another that they can no longer share together in what is, after all, the 'Lord's' supper and not man's.

It also follows from this that, where there is any fundamental doctrinal disagreement among Christians, it is very likely to impinge in some way upon this central act of worship. Smaller matters may not affect it, but any important variance most probably will. Therefore, to reach a substantial consensus on the purpose and meaning of the eucharist is rightly described as 'an important stage in progress towards organic unity' (1). To attain agreement here has implications for other doctrinal matters in dispute. It may provide some indications of the way forward in resolving other difficulties. But the introductory paragraph is careful not to claim too much. The consensus attained is said to be 'substantial', not in the sense of 'large-scale' but rather 'with regard to the essentials': i.e., it deals with the fundamental purpose and meaning of the eucharist. The Statement is not therefore intended to be exhaustive and this needs to be borne continually in mind. Nevertheless, the degree of agreement reached by the Commission should be recognized as a significant milestone, especially in the light of past controversy.

The quest for a deeper understanding of the eucharist has had the further goal of seeking to bring the two communions closer together. Consequently it was fully recognized that any consensus would have to be 'consonant with biblical teaching and with the tradition of our common inheritance' (1). These are also the criteria by which the consensus should be judged. The aim has not been to split hairs but to discover the extent to which we can agree. At the same time there has been no hesitation in tackling the subjects that have been most divisive in the past, such as eucharistic sacrifice and the real presence.

To think freshly with an open mind upon theological issues about which we feel deeply is never an easy task. Our convictions are bound up with traditions in which we have been reared. The Statement recognizes the variety of these traditions that seek to express the meaning of the eucharist.

That such variety exists should neither surprise nor alarm us. If so much Christian truth is focussed in this act of worship, then our insights and emphases are sure to be numerous. What is needed is that they should be tested by the criteria already mentioned. Unfortunately, different names that have become customary for describing the eucharist have tended to become party labels. While one term is jealously guarded, others are spurned. Yet very often they express different aspects of the truth that complement each other. For instance, Evangelicals have preferred to speak of 'the Lord's supper' or 'communion', while regarding 'eucharist' as character-istically Anglo-Catholic and therefore suspect. Yet all three expressions are biblically legitimate. Instinctive reactions should not be allowed to obscure clear thinking. The Statement makes the factual comment, 'The eucharist has become the most universally accepted term' (1). For the theologian 'eucharist' also has the practical advantage of providing an adjective, 'eucharistic', which the other terms do not.

EUCHARIST AS MYSTERY

Among several meanings the word 'mystery' has a long tradition of technical use signifying approximately 'God's action in a visible or quasi-sacramental way, whereby the transcendent God communicates with man'. It is in this sense that the present section is entitled 'The Mystery of the Eucharist', for what it sets out to do is to define the essence and heart of the sacrament. However, by reason of the section's character as a general out-line, it inevitably leaves many questions unanswered. In the nature of the case some are not only unanswered but unanswerable.

Perhaps one of the main reasons for theological confusion with regard to the eucharist has been a lack of awareness of this element of mystery. It has been thought possible nicely to dissect the whole subject with coldly confident analysis. It would have been more timely to heed Augustine's dictum: 'Doctrine is that which hedges about a mystery.' There is in the Statement a phrase that suggests why such an awareness is essential. It indicates a dimension too often forgotten, for it speaks of what Christ does in the eucharist 'through the Holy Spirit' (3). To omit this aspect of the divine activity is to distort the whole picture. Now the New Testament emphasizes the inability of man to fathom the working of the Spirit. 'The wind blows where it wills, and you hear the sound of it, but you do not know whence it comes or whither it goes; so it is with every one who is born of the Spirit' (John 3:8). The Spirit, like the wind, is completely beyond the control and comprehension of man. What is true for the new birth is also true for the eucharist, since the same Spirit is operative in both.

Furthermore, this working of the Spirit implies a dynamism which knits together 'the whole action of the eucharist' (3). So the sacramental pres-ence of Christ is 'given' through bread and wine: the crucified and risen

Lord 'offers himself to his people'. The life of the church is built up, its fellowship strengthened and its mission furthered. This theme is elaborated later in the section on the Presence of Christ, but it is to be noted that it was found necessary to incorporate it in this initial part of the Statement also, where the essential meaning of the eucharist is summarised. A clear grasp of this working of the Spirit will preserve us from too static a view of the eucharist, a tendency only too common in much eucharistic theology. All that having been said, the element of mystery remains; indeed, it is heightened by this awareness of the Spirit's role.

EUCHARISTIC SACRIFICE

If there was one subject that epitomised the tearing apart of Catholic and Protestant in the sixteenth century it was the sacrifice of the mass. Cranmer wrote, 'The papistical priests have taken upon them to be Christ's successors, and to make such an oblation and sacrifice as never creature made but Christ alone, neither he made the same any more times than once, and that was by his death upon the cross.'[1] The Council of Trent pronounced an anathema upon those who would deny the offering of Christ to God in the mass or that the mass was propitiatory.[2] To what extent there may have been mutual misunderstanding is debatable, but that the rift was great is undeniable, and it was a rift in which the Church of England was clearly set on the Protestant side over against the Church of Rome. With these harshly defined positions behind us, what hope had our Commission of reaching a consensus on this thorny matter?

There could hardly be a more explicit emphasis on the finality of the atoning work of Christ. His redeeming death and resurrection are firmly placed in history (5). The emphasis of the writer to the Hebrews upon the 'once for all' nature of Christ's sacrifice[3] is taken up and spelled out. 'There can be no repetition or addition.' 'Any attempt to express a nexus between the sacrifice of Christ and the eucharist must not obscure this fundamental fact of the Christian faith.' It will be observed that the Statement itself conforms to this principle by declining to call the eucharist a sacrifice, although this term has frequently been used by theologians of both communions; it prefers to employ the term 'memorial'. In fact, 'the notion of *memorial* as understood in the passover celebration at the time of Christ— i.e. the making effective in the present of an event in the past—has opened the way to a clearer understanding of the relationship between Christ's sacrifice and the eucharist. The eucharistic memorial is no mere calling to mind of a past event or of its significance, but the church's effectual proclamation of God's mighty acts' (5). The implication is clear. It is not that

[1] *The True and Catholic Doctrine and Use of the Sacrament of the Lord's Supper,* p. 232 (Thynne 1907).

[2] Denzinger 1751, 1753.

[3] Heb. 7:27; 9:12, 26, 28; 10:10.

16

sacrificial language is wholly out of place in eucharistic theology, but that an unguarded use of it has tended to suggest a denial of the finality of the atonement. The members of the Commission have set their face strongly against any such denial. After all, the New Testament writers in employing a rich variety of terms significantly do not call the eucharist a sacrifice (nor indeed do they call the church's ministers priests). Nevertheless, by the second century the application of sacrificial language to the eucharist was taking place. In all probability such language was from a scriptural standpoint entirely unobjectionable.

However, this language of sacrifice, when transferred to the eucharist, has proved in the centuries since then to be a slippery slope. By 1500 the change of terminology had led to a change of theology. Much of what Kung has called 'the valid demands of the Reformers' has now been met by the Church of Rome in the new Eucharistic Prayers, though even in these there remain echoes of the Pre-Reformation language of eucharistic sacrifice. However, the present Statement avoids any suggestion of 're-presenting' Christ's death. What is made present is not the historical sacrifice of Christ itself, but the efficacy of it—'the making effective in the present of an event in the past'(5). There is no biblical warrant for any supra-temporal interpretation of the cross which circumvents its historical finality.

There is a further commendable emphasis in the Statement, which is the more noteworthy for being a deliberate change from what was said in the Venice working paper *Church and Eucharist.* The Venice document stated: 'Christ's whole life, culminating in his death on the Cross, was the one true perfect and sufficient sacrifice for the sins of the whole world.' In contrast the Statement says, 'Christ's death on the cross, the culmination of his whole life of obedience, was the one, perfect and sufficient sacrifice for the sins of the world' (5). The contrast here is obvious. The Venice Paper makes Christ's death merely the high point of obedience and it is the obedience which is the sacrifice. The Statement makes Christ's obedience the necessary qualification and pre-condition for his death, and it is his death which is the sacrifice. How we understand the sacrifice of Christ will inevitably affect our understanding of the eucharist.

Protestant theology has sometimes tended to isolate the death of Christ from his life, resurrection and ascension. But the cross cannot be understood in isolation. Without that whole life of obedience preceding it the cross could not have been an atoning sacrifice. Only the righteous could make an offering for the unrighteous and so bring men back to God (1 Pet. 3:18). In this way is Christ's life of obedience fundamental to the cross. The resurrection and ascension relate no less closely to the cross, for they are God's seal that the cross spelt victory and that the same Christ now reigns. Consequently, while rightly locating the atonement in the death of Christ, the Statement continues: 'Christ instituted the eucharist as a memorial of the totality of God's reconciling action in him.' The bread and wine are the sacrament of his death, but Jesus said, 'Do this in remembrance of me'— of *me,* that is of the incarnate, crucified, raised and ascended Lord.

This section concludes with a summary of what the church does in the eucharist. We have seen the Statement's stress upon the finality of Christ's atoning sacrifice. The fact that the benefits of the passion are made effectively available evokes a response of gratitude and self-offering. The expression used here is that the church 'enters into the movement of his self-offering.' The precise meaning of this phrase must be understood in the light of the whole paragraph. Clearly it is saying more than a fresh commitment in response to God's love. This is not an addition to or repetition of or confusion with what happened on the cross. A glance back historically may clarify the issue. Dom Gregory Dix shows how the understanding of man's self-offering came to be polarised in the sixteenth century.

> "The old concept of the oblation was that Christ offers His perfect oblation of Himself to the Father, and that the earthly church as His Body enters into His eternal priestly act by the eucharist. Cranmer deliberately sought to substitute for this the idea that *we* offer to God *ourselves, our souls and bodies'*.''[1]

That 'old concept' is now set aside by what the Statement has already said concerning the finality of the atoning sacrifice. On the other hand, Cranmer's position, at least as here interpreted by Dix, is not sufficiently related to the work of Christ. Christ's offering of himself to the Father provides a pattern for sacrificial self-offering by us; but it does more than that. It is also God's inescapable demand upon us for our self-offering and the eucharist communicates the demand to us. In this sense the church 'enters into the movement of his self-offering'(5)[2].

To the question, 'What can we offer at the eucharist?', the authors of *Growing into Union* give this answer:

> "Not mere bread and wine—even the term 'offertory' sounds an odd note; not merely 'the fruit of our lips'; not merely undefined 'spiritual sacrifices'; not merely ourselves, considered apart from Christ; not even ourselves in Christ, if that is seen in separation from our feeding on Christ; but ourselves as reappropriated by Christ. If the sacrament is to communicate to us afresh the benefits of Christ's passion, then we must reaffirm quickly that it also communicates to us the demands of it. It may be good liturgically to express our self-offering as responsive to God's grace (by putting the prayer of self-oblation after communion), but there is no real time sequence to be represented."[3]

---

[1] *The Shape of the Liturgy,* Dacre Press (1945) p.666.

[2] The participation in the benefits and the 'entry into the movement of his self-offering' are not in this sentence related narrowly to the eucharistic *prayer* (as is the memorial of Christ's death), but they are simply two among several universally acknowledged features of the whole eucharistic celebration. These two are to be related especially to reception of communion (see the quotation from *Growing into Union* which follows).

[3] Buchanan et al., S.P.C.K. (1970) pp. 59-60. Appendix 4 to *Growing into Union* on 'Eucharistic Sacrifice' by Michael Green and E. L. Mascall, an 'interim agreement' between an Evangelical and an Anglo-Catholic, has marked affinity with the present Statement.

Undoubtedly many things are left unsaid in this section, though it rules out either overtly or at least implicitly many expressions of eucharistic sacrifice which could and have been made. Those that are not ruled out of court by the Statement are not necessarily denied but may be viewed in different ways. They must rank as either peripheral in importance or clumsy and unhelpful in their formulation. For this document claims to be a 'substantial agreement', a consensus on what is fundamental to our understanding of the eucharist.

EUCHARISTIC PRESENCE

Such a variety of meanings has in the past been attached to the word 'presence' that the reader is well advised to approach this section of the Statement with the greatest caution. If he were to fasten on individual sentences without a careful examination of the entire section, he might distort the argument. The section must be seen as a whole. This caution is the more necessary because the Evangelical, for instance, may find his eye lighting upon occasional expressions of strong sacramental language. Thus the opening sentence which speaks of 'the bread and wine which, in this mystery, become his body and blood' (6), was the very sentence which Bishop Butler quoted in the *Times* of 8th September, 1971 soon after the Windsor meeting and before the whole Statement was made public. He commented, 'The commission is very explicit on this real presence.' But, without the full Statement to hand, it inevitably caused some concern. Now that the section can be read as a whole the meaning the Commission gives to the 'real presence' can be established with certainty.

There is no question of a crude material presence here. Our physical bodies are fed in the eucharist by bread and wine. But what Christ offers to his people is not simply bread and wine, 'not mere signs' (9): they are his body and blood. He 'gives himself sacramentally in the body and blood of his paschal sacrifice' and this he does as 'the Lord present at the right hand of the Father, and therefore transcending the sacramental order' (7). By the gracious initiative of God something profound occurs by which the life of Christ is transmitted to the members of his body.

The footnote to paragraph 6 concerning transubstantiation shows the suspicion of contemporary Roman Catholic theology for the philosophical ideas of substance and accidents. The word should be seen as 'affirming the *fact* of Christ's presence and of the mysterious and radical change which takes place.' It is no longer used to define *how* this change occurs. All this is a factual statement without any value judgement. No attempt is made to determine whether the transubstantiation denounced in Article XXVIII as 'repugnant to the plain words of Scripture' is the same as that which the Council of Trent confidently affirmed. If the term has had to undergo modification in its usage by Catholic theologians, it would seem appropriate to discard it. However much it were to be re-interpreted, its retention could only prove a major obstruction to Anglicans.

Much of the misunderstanding can be avoided once the rigid fixing of two moments in the eucharistic action is laid aside. In the past consecration and communion have been regarded as clearly identifiable at a particular point of time, each of the two clearly separated from the other. When the first moment, consecration, was understood as effecting transubstantiation in isolation from the act of communion, it was not surprising that the Reformers objected. For instance, Article XXVIII states: 'The Sacrament of the Lord's Supper was not by Christ's ordinance reserved, carried about, lifted up, or worshipped.' The sacrament was intended to be received as the immediate culmination of the one liturgical action. 'The Lord's words at the last supper, "Take and eat; this is my body", do not allow us to dissociate the gift of the presence and the act of sacramental eating' (9).

At this point we can see more clearly the significance of Cranmer's emphasis upon the association of the presence of Christ with the eating and drinking. This has become a mainstream Anglican tradition, expressed not only in the leading divines of the sixteenth and seventeenth centuries, but also in the language of the Prayer Book Communion service: 'Grant that we receiving these thy creatures of bread and wine, in accordance with thy Son's holy institution . . . may be partakers of his most blessed body and blood'. In modern Anglican liturgies the point is made slightly differently. Whilst there is more preparedness to use the terms 'body' and 'blood' for the elements, there is less emphasis upon a 'moment' of consecration than there has been for the last four centuries. Granted that Anglicans from Jewel onwards did not believe in transubstantiation, yet they did believe there was a moment of consecration, and in this the Puritans at the Savoy Conference were at one with them. The consecration was regarded as an action whereby God set apart bread and wine for their holy use, which might be called trans-signification. But it had reception wholly in view, and was the overture to it. In the rites of the last decade, it is more usual to see the setting apart as effected by the Eucharistic Prayer as a whole, and the idea of a 'moment' has passed.

Nevertheless, even if a precise 'moment' of consecration cannot be isolated, yet in logic there are still what we may call two 'moments' in the eucharist. There must be created a theological context within which we can safely affirm that we are celebrating the Lord's supper, carrying out his command, and not simply having a secular meal of bread and wine. The contextualising is done by the Thanksgiving, or Eucharistic, Prayer. This, in quite objective terms, enables the elements to be treated as the sacramental means of conveying the body and blood of Christ to the worshippers, and does so independently of the state of heart of the particular individuals gathered. The bread and wine thus 'become' the appointed means i.e. his body and and blood. And within the liturgical context, and with a view to reception, it is proper to call them by these terms, as our Lord did.

It is important to emphasize the objectivity of this first logical 'moment'. Catholics have always feared that the Protestant emphasis upon faith at the point of reception, i.e. the second 'moment', delivered the whole rite over to subjectivity. By apparently making the gift of God dependent upon man's faith and not God's grace, Protestants have seemed to make the presence of Christ to be almost at man's beck and call. Hence the Statement asserts that Christ's presence 'does not depend on the individual's faith in order to be the Lord's real gift of himself to his church' (8). So long as the eucharistic action is seen as a whole, this logical order of Christ's 'offering to the believer awaiting his welcome' (8) presents no difficulties. It only becomes suspect when a severance is made between a consecration and reception. Christ offers *himself* to the believer and awaits his welcome. He does not offer bare signs of bread and wine. 'The Bread which we break is a partaking of the Body of Christ; and likewise the Cup of Blessing is a partaking of the Blood of Christ' (Article XXVIII. cf. 1 Cor. 10: 16, 17). The sacramental bread and wine effect what they signify.

Paragraph 8 says that when the offering to men of the sacramental body and blood of the Saviour is 'met by faith, a life-giving encounter results.' Jesus told the Jews, 'Unless you eat the flesh of the Son of man and drink his blood you have no life in you' (John 6: 53). Believing in Jesus, coming to him and feeding upon him are closely interrelated in this sixth chapter of John's Gospel. So to feed in faith is a life-giving encounter. From his presence in the eucharist arises a 'personal relationship between Christ and the faithful'. But to eat and drink unworthily cannot result in any such relationship. If to the unbelieving the sacrament brings judgment, not life (1 Cor. 11:27-30), there must be a distinction within this mystery of the eucharist at the point of reception. One welcomes, another rejects the offer of Christ. Granted this distinction, the same offer has still been made in both instances.

The words of Jesus, 'This is my body', 'This is my blood' set a pattern of realist language in eucharistic theology. To suppose this was the prerogative of Catholic tradition only is to fly in the face of history. In Protestant and Reformed theology also there has always been a tradition of this nature. Zwinglianism was very much a minority opinion and generally repudiated. Calvin is a striking example of one who gives objective content to the sacrament. He speaks of 'the sacred Supper, where Christ offers himself to us with all his blessings, and we receive him in faith.'

"I am not satisfied with the view of those who, while acknowledging that we have some kind of communion with Christ, only make us partakers of the Spirit, omitting all mention of flesh and blood."

"We infer from the exhibition of the symbol that the thing itself is exhibited. For unless we would charge God with deceit, we will never presume to say that he holds forth an empty symbol."[1]

[1] Institutes IV 17. 5, 7, 10. Cf. *Short Treatise on the Lord's Supper*, II, where this theme is fully elaborated.

'Exhibited' means that it is presented and offered to the communicant. If Calvin's eucharistic teaching is occasionally obscure, perhaps because he constantly acknowledges it to be a mystery, yet the realist language is unequivocally there.

The Westminster Confession of Faith, whilst categorically denying any material presence of Christ in the elements, nevertheless fully justifies this realist language.

> "There is in every sacrament a spiritual relation, or sacramental union, between the sign and the thing signified; whence it comes to pass, that the names and effects of the one are attributed to the other."[1]

Richard Baxter's *Reformed Liturgy* included this prayer:

> "Sanctify these thy creatures of bread and wine, which, according to thy institution and command, we set apart to this holy use, that they may be sacramentally the body and blood of thy Son Jesus Christ."

Gregory Dix regarded Baxter's liturgy as 'a whole stage nearer to the catholic tradition' than Cranmer's, because of the essentially Calvinist theology that lies behind it.[2]

Because others have seemed to read into biblical language concerning the sacraments a false sacramentalism, Protestants have sometimes been loth to use even biblical phraseology lest they thereby appeared to be endorsing a questionable eucharistic theology. A reaction, however understandable, against a false position is not the happiest starting-point for obtaining a clear grasp of the comprehensive teaching of scripture. Our aim should be to ensure that both eucharistic doctrine and eucharistic language are 'consonant with biblical teaching' (1) and do exact justice to the balance of scriptural truth.

CONCLUSION

It will be clear from what has been said concerning the quest for agreement on the fundamental issues in eucharistic theology that there are a number of questions that have not been tackled. The Commission is convinced that it should be possible to resolve 'any remaining points of disagreement' by following 'the principles here established' (12). It is important to spell out some of these 'points of disagreement' for, though they are not at the heart of the eucharist, they are none the less matters of great concern. Because the Commission was dealing with doctrine, no great attention has been paid in the text to eucharistic practice or the liturgical forms by which doctrine is expressed. Allusion has already been made in this Commentary to features in the new Eucharistic Prayers that create problems for an Evangelical. How far our current liturgical texts express the doctrinal

[1] XXVII. 2.
[2] Op. Cit. p. 677.

22

consensus of the Commission has yet to be judged. The practice of reservation, so wide-spread in Roman Catholic circles and also among a minority of Anglicans, is a controversial matter in the Church of England: inferences concerning this practice can be drawn from the Statement, but they are not explicit within it. Again, Protestants have always insisted on administration in both kinds, wine as well as bread. There are signs of this reappearing in the church of Rome, but these are not yet widespread. The practice of votive masses, especially of requiems, also needs examination in the light of this Statement. It should be possible today to examine these controversial topics a little more dispassionately than in the sixteenth century. Finally, it should be noted that agreement in eucharistic doctrine does not of itself bring official intercommunion into sight, as there remains, among other obstacles, the question of the relation of the eucharist to the ministry. This question is not being shelved, but is sure to engage the Commission's attention as it concentrates upon the doctrine of the ministry in the coming year.

This consensus should cause Roman Catholics to re-evaluate the relation between their current eucharistic theology and that contained in the dogmatic decrees of the Council of Trent. An Anglican must ask to what extent a Roman Catholic still feels bound by those decrees even when his present theology appears to have moved on or away from them. The underlying question of authority is never far below the surface. For many Anglicans this agreement could well provoke a fresh study of their eucharistic practice. Is the Holy Communion as central to the church's life as scripture warrants? Or has a fear of a false sacramentalism led to an under-estimation of its importance?

It is to be noted that the Commission's claim to have reached 'substantial agreement' (12) concludes a document that omits any reference to adoration, reservation or benediction in connection with the sacrament. Moreover, the consensus concerns the *purpose* as well as the meaning of the sacrament (1). This suggests that further enquiry should be directed not so much at finding ways of validating or legitimising current devotional practices as to asking more penetratingly to what end our Lord instituted the eucharist.

What the Commission's Statement puts forward needs to be reviewed in a broader ecumenical context. It is only the opinion of a small Commission and is submitted for the widest possible consideration. However, the Commission is made up of representatives officially appointed by both churches. Is it a compromise or a straw in the wind for a more hopeful future? Has the ground between the Roman Catholic and Anglican communions been narrowed? Much, of course, will depend on how far it receives general acceptance, but, in the opinion of one participant at least, it is a hopeful sign.

GROVE BOOKLETS ON MINISTRY AND WORSHIP

Published one each month—24 (or more) pages. Titles asterisked are in second edition or a reprint. Cost **25p.** Nos. 4 and 11 are not available. Send for catalogue.

*1. **The Anglican-Roman Catholic Agreement on the Eucharist** by Julian W. Charley

*2. **Ministry in the Local Church** by P. A. Crowe, A. R. Henderson and J. I. Packer

*3. **Baptismal Discipline (Revised Edition)** by Colin Buchanan

*5. **A Service of Thanksgiving and Blessing** by C. H. B. Byworth and J. A. Simpson. (Also Service Sheet only **5p** or **45p** per dozen and Certificate **4p**)

6. **Informal Liturgy** by Trevor Lloyd

*7. **The Church and the Gifts of the Spirit** by John Goldingay

*8. **Communion, Confirmation and Commitment (Revised Edition)** by C. H. B. Byworth

*9. **Patterns of Sunday Worship** by Colin Buchanan

*10. **A Guide to Series 3** by Peter E. Dale

*12. **The Language of Series 3** by David L. Frost

13. **What Priesthood has the Ministry?** by J. M. R. Tillard

14. **Recent Liturgical Revision in the Church of England** by Colin Buchanan

14A. **Supplement for 1973-4 to Recent Liturgical Revision in the Church of England** by Colin Buchanan

15. **Institutions and Inductions** by Trevor Lloyd

16. **Alternative Eucharistic Prayers** by Derek Billings

17. **Evangelicals and the Ordination of Women.** Edited by Colin Craston

18. **Community, Prayer and the Individual** by Peter R. Akehurst

19. **Agapes and Informal Eucharists** by Trevor Lloyd

20. **A case for Infant Baptism** by Colin Buchanan

21. **Evangelistic Services** by Michael H. Botting

22. **Agreement on the Doctrine of the Ministry** by Julian W. Charley

23. **A Modern Liturgical Bibliography** by John E. Tiller

24. **Infant Baptism under Cross-Examination** by David Pawson and Colin Buchanan

25. **Send us out** by Peter E. Dale

26. **Music for the Parish** by Sidney Green and Gordon Ogilvie

27. **Ministry and Death** by Trevor Lloyd

28. **Liturgy and Death** by Trevor Lloyd

29. **The Ordinal and its Revision** by Peter Toon

30. **Liturgy and Creation** by Peter R. Akehurst

31. **Christian Education on Sunday Mornings.** Edited by Charles Hutchins

32. **Inaugural Services.** Edited by Colin Buchanan

33. **Knowing God through the Liturgy** by Peter Toon

34. **Modern Roman Catholic Worship: The Mass** by Nicholas Sagovsky

35. **Drama in Worship** by Andy Kelso

36. **Praying Aloud Together** by Peter R. Akehurst

37. **The Liturgy for Infant Baptism (Series 3)** by Colin Buchanan

*38. **Open to God** by Tom Walker

39. **Worship and Silence** by Margaret Harvey

40. **Freedom in a Framework** by Richard More

41. **Keeping Holy Week** by Peter R. Akehurst (January 1976) **(30p)**

42. **Christian Healing in the Parish** by Michael Botting (February 1976) **(30p)**

43. **Modern Roman Catholic Worship: Other Services** by Nicholas Sagovsky (April 1976) **(30p)**